Listening to Trees

George Nakashima, Woodworker

WORDS BY Holly Thompson   PICTURES BY Toshiki Nakamura

NEAL PORTER BOOKS
HOLIDAY HOUSE / NEW YORK

My Father

I am so happy that Holly Thompson has decided to write a book about my father, George Nakashima. As his daughter, I never realized that my father was doing anything different from what ordinary fathers do, nor that the houses he built were anything unusual . . . until I grew up, went to college, studied architecture and Japanese, went to Japan . . . and then came home again!

My father was very loving but also very strict, and he would not tolerate disobedience or, oftentimes, differences of opinion after I came back to work for him. He had slowly built his own world, which my parents used to call "Mira Land," perhaps wanting me to feel at home on the first property they owned; strongly believed that "Small Is Beautiful"; and always lived where he worked. His clients became friends and friends became clients, a relationship based on mutual respect. Sometimes his artist friends would trade their work for furniture; sometimes his doctor or photographer friends would trade their services for furniture, which made us all very grateful to one another.

Most of all, my father loved the forests and the land that gave us sustenance, and the peace and quiet of the environment he built over the years. He believed in hard, honest work, made from the trees he respected and loved, carefully designed and crafted by hand tools. Today, we still use most of the machines he purchased during his lifetime, even though they are not very efficient compared to modern machines. Our way of working requires total concentration, akin to deep meditation, and cannot be done quickly. This is not just making furniture but a way of life, a way to pay respects to our natural environment and the people who work together to create "antiques of the future," not just "machines for living" (as one architect thought of houses and furniture!).

So we invite you on a journey to discover who George Nakashima was and why he inspires us, hoping that he will continue to inspire generations to come. I hope that you will enjoy this adventure as much as I have!

Mira Nakashima

a boy
catches his breath
at the timberline

George Nakashima felt at home in the woods—among firs that speared the sky and stunted evergreens clinging to mountaintops.

a pack
a pair of shoes
worn completely through

He loved hiking trails in the Cascade Range
and Olympic Mountains, climbing from pass
to pass, always eager for the next vista.

*forests
spread out below
a vast sea of trees*

Admirer of trees,
George studied forestry, then
switched to architecture. But in summers,
he worked the railroads, staying close
to the wilderness he loved.

sunlight
on tatami
doors open to winter

As a young man, George boarded a ship to Japan, land of his ancestors, to work for an American architect in Tokyo. He stayed in his mother's family home—a sturdy old farmhouse with beams and posts of fine zelkova wood.

*two friends
on a veranda
quiet cups of tea*

Sometimes George traveled out of the city to visit forests and catch the fragrance of blooms.

With an architect friend,
he toured temples, shrines,
and teahouses.

He saw power in simplicity and beauty in
unfinished wood. And at work, he drew
plans mixing traditional with modern,
concrete with wood.

breeze
of oleander
silence calms the mind

One job sent George to India to build a dormitory at an ashram. George took charge of design and construction, even crafting the chairs, benches, and tables from teakwood. For two years, George lived a simple life. With daily tasks, meditation, and meals in silence, he was content.

But war was building in Asia, and George knew he needed to return to Tokyo, then Seattle.

*identical rings
handmade of silver
for a life together*

In Tokyo, George met
Japanese American teacher
Marion, and after they'd each safely
returned to the US, they married.

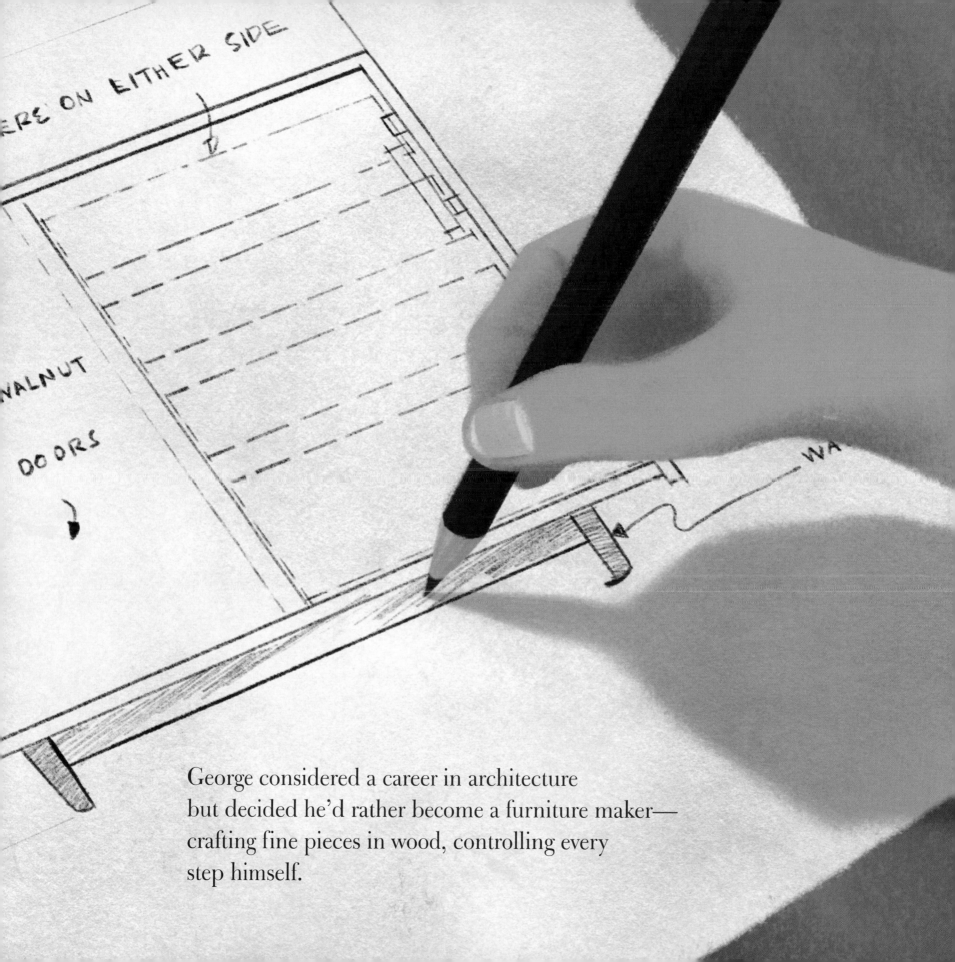

George considered a career in architecture
but decided he'd rather become a furniture maker—
crafting fine pieces in wood, controlling every
step himself.

parents, children
grandparents, cousins
numbered, no longer free

George set up a workshop and
began growing a future with Marion
and their new daughter, Mira. But life was
turned upside down when war between Japan
and America began.

The US government reacted with
racism, and people of Japanese ancestry—
innocent Americans like George, Marion, and baby
Mira—were sent away to prison camps.

two men
with scrap lumber
aiming for perfection

At the Minidoka prison camp, families
coped in harsh conditions. Marion
cared for their baby girl.

George was assigned to improve housing and make furniture, and that's how he met Gentaro Hikogawa, a carpenter who taught him more about the ways of Japanese tools and the art of Japanese joinery. In such a bleak and hopeless place, George was comforted by the discipline of woodworking.

*a chance
for freedom
worth dealing with chickens*

After a year, George and his family could be released from Minidoka—but only if they were sponsored to move east.

NORTH DAKOTA

SOUTH DAKOTA

MINNESOTA

WISCONSIN

MICHIGAN

MAINE

VERMONT

NEW HAMPSHIRE

NEW YORK

MASSACHUSETTS

RHODE ISLAND

CONNECTICUT

PENNSYLVANIA

NEW JERSEY

DELAWARE

MARYLAND

NEBRASKA

IOWA

ILLINOIS

INDIANA

OHIO

WEST VIRGINIA

VIRGINIA

COLORADO

KANSAS

MISSOURI

KENTUCKY

NORTH CAROLINA

TENNESSEE

SOUTH CAROLINA

OKLAHOMA

ARKANSAS

ALABAMA

GEORGIA

MISSISSIPPI

TEXAS

LOUISIANA

FLORIDA

The architect that George had worked for in Japan owned a family farm in Pennsylvania, so the Nakashimas traveled east to live and work at his farm.

*stones
in a wheelbarrow
hauled to grow a house*

But George had no interest in farming—he was a woodworker! After the war, the Nakashimas rented a house where George created a workshop in a garage.

When George had a chance to trade labor for some south-facing land he liked, he and Marion, with little Mira, began building their own workshop, then their own house—stone by stone, plank by plank.

*workshops
lumber sheds
and a home for a growing family*

The Nakashimas became a woodworking family—
deep in the hills of Bucks County, amid hardwood
forests of walnut, ash, maple, poplar, and oak. Marion
was manager. Mira and new brother Kevin helped.

As a family, the Nakashimas sold George's fine furniture to buyers from around the country.

a root
sawn into a slab
an elegant end table

When an old tree falls, or is cut,
there is timber. George loved timber—
the grain in fruitwood, burls, dark
heartwood, and light sapwood.

He collected wood—unused trunks
from fallen giants—decades, centuries
old. What could he craft with each?

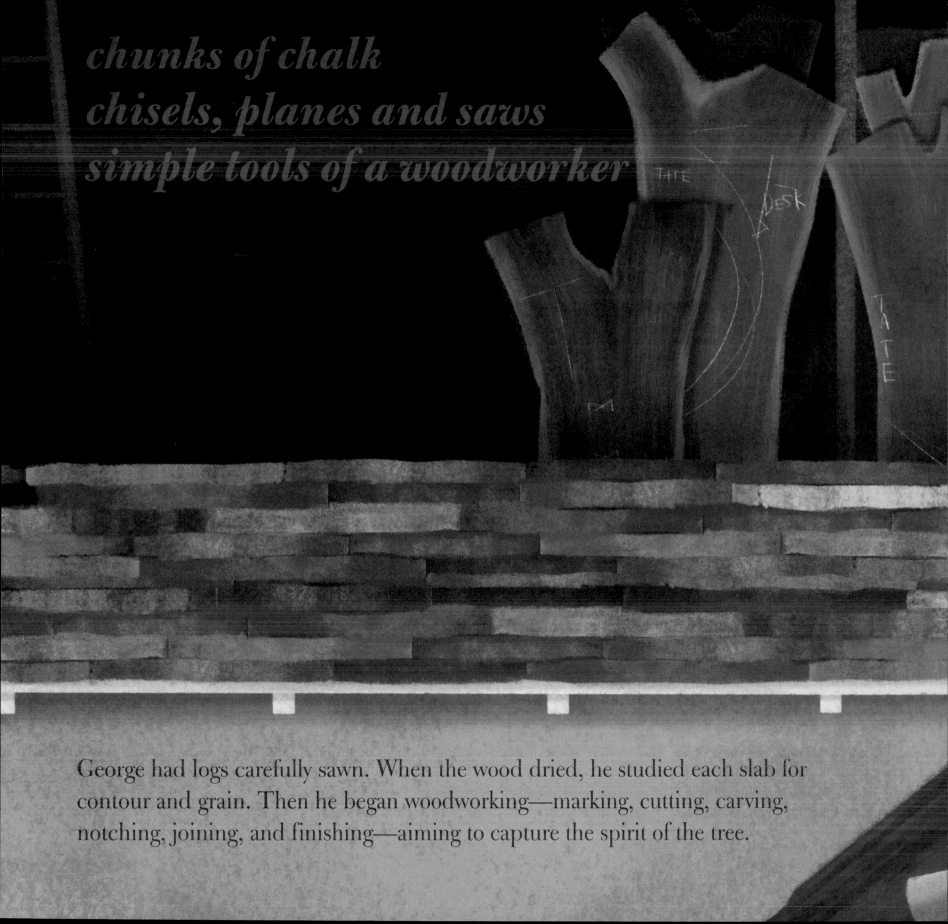

chunks of chalk
chisels, planes and saws
simple tools of a woodworker

George had logs carefully sawn. When the wood dried, he studied each slab for contour and grain. Then he began woodworking—marking, cutting, carving, notching, joining, and finishing—aiming to capture the spirit of the tree.

two boards
book-matched and notched
awaiting butterflies

George blended natural shapes with architectural lines, American Shaker design with traditional Japanese design. He used butterfly joints—inlays shaped like butterfly wings—to span weak spots or between "book-matched" boards. He believed in giving a tree a second life of dignity and strength.

a log
sawn into boards
a dream for the world

Late in his life, George bought an
enormous log of American walnut. With its
huge boards, George could do something
unusual. But what should that be?

half a ton
ten feet across
a table for peace on earth

George decided to create enormous
altar tables—one for each continent
of the world. He hoped people
would gather around those
altars and make peace.

George's first altar table
was so huge a flatbed truck
transported it to its cathedral
home in New York City.

a father
trusts his children
to carry on the craft

George made furniture until the end of his life.
Although he died before all six peace tables
were completed, his peace project continues.

Could the workshop, tucked amid the forests that George loved, survive without George? Yes, his children decided. The woodworkers agreed. Their patient craft continues in the George Nakashima way—listening, marking, cutting, carving, notching, joining, and finishing—giving noble trees new life.

A Note from the Author

I first learned about George Nakashima through my father, who loved wood. His visit to the George Nakashima Woodworkers complex was transformative, and he loved to study the photographs in Nakashima's book *The Soul of a Tree*. My father lovingly crafted many items in wood, and he designed the family dining areas with cherrywood cabinets. I grew up appreciating wood. After moving to Japan, I fell in love with the craftsmanship of traditional Japanese wood houses, and I began to seek out ancient trees. I have visited many 1,000-year-old trees.

Once when I was in Shikoku researching the Japanese American sculptor Isamu Noguchi, my friend and renowned translator Cathy Hirano took me to the George Nakashima Memorial Gallery, connected to a furniture company that makes furniture designed by George Nakashima. As I learned more about him, I knew I wanted to write a picture book biography about his woodworking ways. I later visited the Nakashima complex in New Hope, Pennsylvania, to discuss my ideas with Mira and Kevin, George Nakashima's children, and I was fortunate to receive their encouragement.

I chose the haibun form for this story about George Nakashima because haibun is often used for journeys. Nakashima traveled far and wide in his lifetime. Haibun originated in Japan and was popularized by poet Matsuo Bashō (1644–1694). Bashō wrote haibun as he meandered the country, most famously as he traveled around northern Japan on foot for five months. Haibun is a combination of haiku (*hai*ku) and prose (*bun*shō). In haibun, the haiku and the prose depend on each other to gain meaning. Each expands the other. Sometimes the haiku is placed at the beginning of the prose (or prose poem), sometimes at the end, and sometimes prose and haiku alternate. Haibun originated in Japan, but today, haibun are written in many languages.

I'm so grateful to everyone who has made this picture book journey possible, most especially Mira Nakashima and George Nakashima Woodworkers.

Holly Thompson

George Nakashima Timeline

1905 Born May 24, George Katsutoshi Nakashima (中島勝寿) in Spokane, Washington, to Issei (first generation) parents

1917-23 Active in Boy Scouts, earns rank of Eagle, hikes in Cascade Range and Olympic Mountains

1925 Visits relatives in Japan

1929 Earns BArch degree from University of Washington; during year abroad earns diploma at École des Beaux-Arts, Fontainebleu, France

1930 Earns MArch degree from Massachusetts Institute of Technology

1931-33 Becomes an architectural designer, Long Island State Park Commission

1933-34 Lives in Paris

George as Boy Scout

1934-36 Moves to Japan; works as architect in Tokyo firm of Czech American architect Antonin Raymond; lives with mother's family in Kamata (now part of Tokyo); travels in Kyoto, Nara, and Ise with architect Junzō Yoshimura; projects include the summer home of Antonin Raymond and Saint Paul's Catholic Church, both in Karuizawa

George at MIT graduation

1936-39 Moves to Pondicherry, India, to design, construct, and furnish dormitory at ashram of Sri Aurobindo; becomes a disciple, receives Sanskrit name Sundarananda—"one who delights in beauty"

1939 Returns to Tokyo; works in new architectural firm of a former colleague; meets Japanese American Marion Sumire Okajima (1912–2004)

1940 Becomes engaged to Marion; returns to US

1941 Marries Marion; begins making furniture in basement workshop in Seattle for André Ligné

1942 Daughter Mira Shizuko Nakashima born

1942-43 Nakashima family incarcerated at Minidoka prison camp in Idaho; George meets Issei carpenter Gentaro Kenneth Hikogawa, learns more techniques of traditional Japanese woodworking and joinery

Woodworkers at Minidoka prison camp

1943 Released from Minidoka; family moves to Raymond Farm in New Hope, Pennsylvania

1944-46 Makes furniture in garage workshop for Knoll Associates

1947 Moves to Aquetong Road property in New Hope and gradually builds a home and workshop

1947-90 Develops his craft-furniture business; designs and builds fifteen buildings and their furniture on his property

George in his workshop

1952 Awarded Gold Craftsmanship Medal, American Institute of Architects

1954 Son Kevin Katsuya Nakashima born (1954–2020)

1964 Joins Sanuki Minguren group in Takamatsu, Kagawa Prefecture, Japan, collaborating with local artisans inventing new ways to blend traditional craftsmanship with modern ways of life

1968 First of eight prominent Odakyu Department Store shows of Nakashima's furniture held in Tokyo

1974 Completes commission for former Governor Nelson A. Rockefeller—crafts 200 pieces for Rockefeller's Japanese-style home, designed by Junzō Yoshimura in Pocantico Hills, New York

Mira and Kevin

1979 Awarded and given title of Fellow, American Craft Council, New York

1980 Awarded Gold Medal and named Japanese American of the Biennium, Japanese American Citizens League, San Francisco

1981 Writes *The Soul of a Tree*, published by Kodansha International

1983 Awarded the Order of the Sacred Treasure by the emperor and Japanese government

1986 Installs first peace altar at Cathedral Church of Saint John the Divine, New York City

1989 Exhibits retrospective show at the American Craft Museum, New York

1990 Dies June 15

George at work planing

Growth of a Tree

George Nakashima created furniture using lumber from tree trunks, roots, burls, and branches.

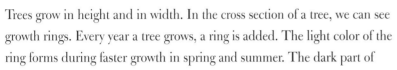

crown—with branches, leaves, fruits/nuts/cones/seeds

trunk

roots

Trees grow in height and in width. In the cross section of a tree, we can see growth rings. Every year a tree grows, a ring is added. The light color of the ring forms during faster growth in spring and summer. The dark part of the ring is formed during slower growth in fall and winter.

growth rings

A tree has outer bark; inner bark; a cambium growing layer; sapwood for moving water up and down the tree; heartwood, which is the dead part of the tree; and a core or pith in the center of the tree. Trees also have a crown of leaves that make food for the tree.

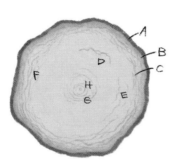

A BARK
B CAMBIUM LAYER
C HEART WOOD BEGINS
D WIND SHAKE
  (Year of The storm)
E WET YEARS
  (open fast growth)
F DRY YEARS
  (Tight slow growth)
G EARLY FAST GROWTH
H PITH

Burls are abnormal rounded growths on trees, and cross sections of burls appear to have buds or "eyes."

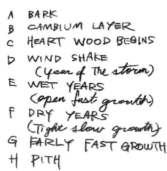

Cross section of a tree diagram and labels from The Soul of a Tree *by George Nakashima.*

Woodworking Process

1. Find lumber: Harvest lumber from selected full-grown trees, sometimes discarded, fallen, or past their prime.

2. Dry the wood: "Sticker" the wood with wooden spacers to air-dry for several years before kiln-drying. After kiln-drying, remove stickers, "dead-pile" the wood, and store in lumber barn.

3. Choose wood for a project: When choosing a board, search for a size that minimizes waste. Then "dress" (finish) a small area and apply water to get an idea of the color, tone, grain, and personality of the wood.

4. Design the furniture: Measure for size and thickness of the project. Then roughly chalk the cut lines on the wood. Photograph and send to the client, with a section of the "dressed" and moistened wood. After client approval, draw the design to be elegantly simple.

6. Join: Join the boards, legs, feet, dowels (spokes), arms, and backs.

5. Prepare the wood: Kiln-dry the wood a second time and run it over the joiner and planer. With a pencil, mark the cut lines and trim to size. Remove any rough bark and sand all surfaces. Cut joints, drill holes, or fit butterflies.

7. Finish: Sand the wood many times with finer and finer grit sandpaper before applying tung oil, drying, sanding, and reapplying many coats of oil until final finish is achieved.

Shibui, **wabi,** and **sabi** are Japanese ideas that apply to all Nakashima furniture pieces. In Japanese, *shibui* means astringent, like an unripe persimmon; at Nakashima Woodworkers, *shibui* means the spare use of materials and tight lines. *Wabi* means quiet or solitary, and being solitary enables us to hear a "still, small voice within." *Sabi* means rusty or antique and can describe something elegantly simple.

Adapted from NakashimaWoodworkers.com, courtesy of Mira Nakashima. Quote from George Nakashima.

George Nakashima Furniture

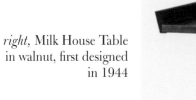

right, Milk House Table in walnut, first designed in 1944

above, Conoid Chair in black walnut and hickory, first designed in 1960

opposite, Reception House dining area with Dining Table in English walnut and eight Conoid Chairs in black walnut

above, Conoid Desk with wych elm burl top

above, Grass-seated Chair in cherry, first designed in 1947

above, Odakyu Cabinet in walnut with cedar asa no ha doors made in Japan, first designed in 1976

above, Plank Coffee Table, designed when George Nakashima received some live-edge boards of walnut in the 1940s

ABOUT THE HAIBUN FORM

Haibun is a form of poetry originating from Japan and popularized by the poet Matsuo Bashō (1644–1694). Bashō wrote haibun as he meandered the country, most famously as he traveled around northern Japan on foot for five months. The collection of haibun from that journey was published as *Oku no hosomichi* (奥の細道) often translated as *Narrow road to the far north* or *Narrow road to the interior*.

Haibun is a combination of haiku (*hai*ku) and prose (*bun*shō). In haibun, the haiku and the prose depend on each other to gain meaning. Each expands the other. Sometimes the haiku is placed at the beginning of the prose (or prose poem), sometimes at the end, and sometimes prose and haiku alternate. Haibun originated in Japan, but today, haibun are written in many languages.

In memory of my father,
who found solace in forests
and working with wood —H.T.

For my father —T.N.

Neal Porter Books

Text copyright © 2024 by Holly Thompson
Illustrations copyright © 2024 by Toshiki Nakamura
All photos copyright © George Nakashima Woodworkers, S.A., New Hope, PA
www.nakashimawoodworkers.com
All Rights Reserved
HOLIDAY HOUSE is registered in the U.S. Patent and Trademark Office.
Printed and bound in June 2024 at Leo Paper, Heshan, China.
The artwork for this book was created with digital tools.
Book design by Jennifer Browne
www.holidayhouse.com
First Edition
10 9 8 7 6 5 4 3 2 1
Library of Congress Cataloging-in-Publication Data is available.

ISBN: 978-0-8234-5049-7 (hardcover)

BIBLIOGRAPHY AND RESOURCES

"Gentaro Kenneth Hikogawa," Densho Encyclopedia. https://encyclopedia.densho.org/Gentaro_Kenneth_Hikogawa.

"George Nakashima," Densho Encyclopedia. https://encyclopedia.densho.org/George_Nakashima.

George Nakashima Memorial Hall (ジョージナカシマ記念館), Takamatsu, Kagawa Prefecture, Japan. https://www.sakurashop.co.jp/memorial_hall.

George Nakashima, Woodworker, film by John Terry Nakashima, 2020. https://nakashimadocumentary.com.

Mira Nakashima, A Place at the Table video. Articulate, April 17, 2019. https://articulateshow.org/videos/mira-nakashima-a-place-at-the-table.

Nakashima, George. *The Soul of a Tree: A Master Woodworker's Reflections.* Kodansha USA, New York, 1981, 2001.

Nakashima, Mira. *Nature Form & Spirit: The Life and Legacy of George Nakashima.* Abrams, New York, 2003.

Nakashima, Mira. *Process Book.* George Nakashima Woodworkers, 2023. https://nakashimawoodworkers.com/accessory/process-book.

Nakashima Woodworkers Furniture Studio, New Hope, Pennsylvania. https://nakashimawoodworkers.com.

Peace Tables, Nakashima Foundation for Peace. https://nakashimafoundation.org/peace-tables-around-the-world.

"The Craftsman: Fulfilling our Need and Nostalgia for Wood." Interview with George Nakashima, photographed by John Loengard, *Life*, Vol. 68, No. 22, pp. 74–78, June 12, 1970.

Thompson, Holly. Conversations with Mira Nakashima and Kevin Nakashima, October 4, 2015; conversations and correspondence with Mira Nakashima 2021–2023.